Farm Pets

Casual Cows

Colleen Dolphin
AUTHOR

C.A. Nobens
ILLUSTRATOR

Consulting Editor, Diane Craig, M.A./Reading Specialist

ABDO
Publishing Company

Published by ABDO Publishing Company, 8000 West 78th Street, Edina, Minnesota 55439.

Printed in the United States of America, North Mankato, Minnesota
052010
092010

 PRINTED ON RECYCLED PAPER

Editor: Liz Salzmann
Content Developer: Nancy Tuminelly
Cover and Interior Design and Production: Colleen Dolphin, Mighty Media
Photo Credits: Corbis Images, Shutterstock

Library of Congress Cataloging-in-Publication Data
Dolphin, Colleen, 1979-
  Casual cows / Colleen Dolphin.
     p. cm. -- (Farm pets)
  ISBN 978-1-61613-369-6
  1. Dairy cattle--Juvenile literature. 2. Cows--Juvenile literature. I. Title.
  SF208.D646 2010
  636.2--dc22
                              2009053104

SandCastle™ Level: Transitional
SandCastle™ books are created by a team of professional educators, reading specialists, and content developers around five essential components—phonemic awareness, phonics, vocabulary, text comprehension, and fluency—to assist young readers as they develop reading skills and strategies and increase their general knowledge. All books are written, reviewed, and leveled for guided reading, early reading intervention, and Accelerated Reader® programs for use in shared, guided, and independent reading and writing activities to support a balanced approach to literacy instruction. The SandCastle™ series has four levels that correspond to early literacy development. The levels are provided to help teachers and parents select appropriate books for young readers.

| Emerging Readers (no flags) | Beginning Readers (1 flag) | Transitional Readers (2 flags) | Fluent Readers (3 flags) |

SandCastle™ would like to hear from you. Please send us your comments and suggestions.
sandcastle@abdopublishing.com

Contents

Cows

Cows are **tame** and friendly. They like to spend the day **munching** on grass. *Cattle* is another word for cows.

A calf is a young cow. A calf stays safe and warm in a barn.

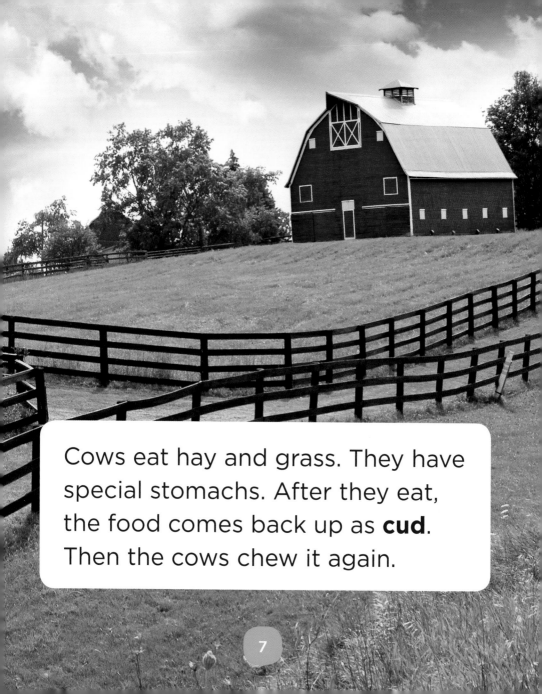

Cows eat hay and grass. They have special stomachs. After they eat, the food comes back up as **cud**. Then the cows chew it again.

Cows need to drink a lot of water each day.

Cows produce a lot of milk. Kayla milks her cow every day. She gets to drink the milk when it's ready.

Ben spends time with his pet cow Chad. Ben talks to Chad while he brushes his coat.

A Cow Story

Anna's cow Sunny
made **delicious** milk.
Everyone who drank it
said it was smooth as silk.

One day Anna decided
to start a milk stand.
She knew people would come
from all over the land!

Anna poured Sunny's milk
and got the stand ready.
She needed some help
so she asked her friend Eddie.

Soon it was opening day and lots of people stood in line. Everyone said that the milk was **divine**!

Did You Know?

* Cows spend about eight hours each day eating.

* One cow makes about 200,000 glasses of milk during its lifetime.

* Cows can smell things that are up to six miles (10 km) away.

* A cow can walk up stairs but cannot walk down them.

* Cows stand up and sit down about 14 times a day.

Cow Quiz

Read each sentence below. Then decide whether it is true or false!

1. Cows do not eat grass.

2. Barns keep cows safe and warm.

3. Cows need to drink a lot of water.

4. Cows produce milk.

5. Anna started a lemonade stand.

Answers: 1. False 2. True 3. True 4. True 5. False

Glossary

cud – food swallowed by a cow that comes back up into the cow's mouth. Then the cow chews it again.

delicious – very pleasing to taste or smell.

divine – wonderful or excellent.

munch – to chew or snack on.

tame – gentle and obedient.

To see a complete list of SandCastle™ books and other nonfiction titles from ABDO Publishing Company, visit www.abdopublishing.com.

8000 West 78th Street, Edina, MN 55439 • 800-800-1312 • fax 952-831-1632